CW00494469

21 Days to Live Life Stronger

Dr Joselyn Sellen

Copyright © 2023 Dr Joselyn Sellen

All rights reserved.

ISBN: 9798396811850

DEDICATION

I would like to dedicate this book to my very good friend, Julie Rose. In 2020, at the age of 47 she was diagnosed with incurable thyroid cancer. As a single mum, with 3 children, all under 15, this diagnosis was devastating. Since that time she has been on a clinical trial with The Royal Marsden Hospital, which so far has given her another 2 years of living and making memories. How long this will last is unknown. Her tenacity and bravery have been an inspiration to many, including me. Julie lives courageously with stage 4 thyroid cancer, and in June 2023 Julie will *once again* participate in the London to Paris 4-day cycle ride to raise money for the Royal Marsden. Julie has inspired many people to live life with purpose, in whatever time they have to live a full life. Julie has taught me not to take life for granted and not to waste time wishing, but to take action to make life meaningful, in the here and now. And you can too.

At the end of this book I ask you a question:

You have one, short, precious life – what will you do with the rest of yours?

Look to those who inspire you, look to those who live bravely, look to those who will not settle for mediocre.

And then decide what exactly *you* want from your one precious life.

You have it within yourself to create the life you want, on your terms. I hope this 21 Days to Live Life Stronger book will help you start this adventure.

CONTENTS

ACKNOWLEDGMENTS

Completing this book would not have been possible without the help and support of a number of people. I would like to thank Liz Taplin, my amazing Coach for her skills in helping me actually finish this book; Suzanne Carrie, for proof-reading and editing (any mistakes are of course mine alone); Andy Dickson and Anthony Davies for reading the manuscript and giving me honest feedback; Julie Rose for the book cover photograph; and Richie Evans for patiently designing the book cover against a hard deadline. I am grateful to everyone who willingly gave their time and expertise freely in pursuit of a worthy cause to raise money for the life-changing research of The Royal Marsden Hospital. I am forever indebted.

And of course my children, Kat and Max; and my Mum and Dad, for believing in me, always.

INTRODUCTION

The purpose of this book is to help you start living your life with more self-awareness, energy, focus and purpose. This 21 Day Live Life Stronger book is separated into six Growth Zones, which are built on each other to help you create a solid foundation for your psychological and emotional wellbeing.

There are many traditional pillars of positive wellbeing, for example, eating well, walking in nature, exercising, connection, good sleep hygiene, good work/life balance and so on. Whilst acknowledging the importance of these pillars, this book focuses more on our psychological wellbeing. This 21 Day Programme is designed to help you understand, strengthen and protect your emotional wellbeing, and to build your resilience. For most people, life is rarely easy and we can spend a long time feeling discontented, unhappy and unfulfilled. I firmly believe that when we understand and take steps to actively protect our psychological health, we are empowering ourselves to better manage the challenges that life throws at us.

If life is full of struggle, doesn't it make sense to build, strengthen and protect your emotional and psychological armoury?

Many people live with anxiety, or ruminate on past events, or feel constantly stressed, or feel debilitating low mood. More often than not, these symptoms are treated by the use of anti-depressants or anti-anxiety medication, which may ease symptoms, but do nothing to treat the underlying causes, and the actual reasons for poor mental health remain intact.

People who suffer such symptoms and conditions can lack understanding of why they feel the way they do, and live alongside a constant inner critic in

1

their own head. The voice of the 'Inner Critic' is quick to put us down; it tells us we are not capable, too stupid, too lazy, too much and more often than not, simply not enough. It tells us we are not lovable enough, not clever enough, not pretty enough, not strong enough; the list really is endless. It is no wonder, when we have a pervasive inner critic, *which we pay attention to*, that our psychological health suffers. We can often speak to ourselves much more cruelly than anyone else ever does, and certainly more so than how we would ever speak to anyone else.

Using healthy positive habits as the starting block for your journey to living life stronger, this book will help you understand your emotional wellbeing and to begin to identify your negative thinking habits. Learning to be self-compassionate and kind to ourselves is one of the most important steps in overcoming the negativity that often pervade our thoughts and emotions when we are experiencing poor mental health.

Many people say they "want to be happy", or they "want to live a life with purpose" or "I want to be the best version of me" but when it comes to doing anything about it, they often don't know where to start. It can feel overwhelming. If you are in that headspace where you think you could feel better, stronger, more resilient, but you simply don't know where to start – then you are in the right place. Read on:

Where Do I Start?

Right here, right now.

When my clients start working with me, they often say they feel 'stuck'. They are often stuck in a rut of domestic chores, family responsibilities, demands of their job and the humdrum of daily life. It can seem like there just is not the time or space to make any kind of lasting change.

It can feel as though there are so many things we need to do in order to be the best version of ourselves. Perhaps you have an inner demon, that inner voice, who is always putting you down, the inner critic can be cruel and keep us very small indeed. Or you may believe that you just don't have it in you; you are destined for a life where you simply don't feel you will ever reach your full potential. Or maybe you know you are not managing your emotions, you fly off the handle and say things in a rage that you don't mean, and end up having to apologise and think "why did I say or do that?", the red mist has come down, and you've been helpless to do anything about it. It's as though you've been taken over by another being! Or maybe you know, *you just know*, that you use unhelpful coping strategies to manage life on a day-to-day basis, and that in all likelihood, these unhelpful habits might just be making life harder and more intolerable. And you have a sinking feeling that 'this is it', until the unhelpful coping strategies are dealt with you are destined to never reach your full potential and never be the best version of you.

I'm here to tell you that this just isn't true. Making lasting change does not have to be an impossible challenge. Taking small and manageable steps on a regular basis is the key to making change happen. This book will guide you through some of the fundamental steps to making change and becoming the best version of you.

When Do I Start?

Now! Even if you start making one small step today, you are making changes to you and how you interact with your world. You are making positive change happen – today. By reading this book and starting to put small actions into place, you are making change happen. I recommend buying yourself a notebook. An inexpensive lined notebook will do just fine. In it you can write, reflect, and journal all the important information that you will learn throughout this book. Through these actions you will develop and increase your self-awareness and see your own personal growth happen before your eyes.

How Do I Start?

By keeping reading, and committing to read one section per day. This book is written so that you can read a daily section which will either be a new learning experience, a task, an insight, or something to reflect on. It is designed for busy people who want to start making their personal growth and development a priority, but don't know where, when or how to start.

If you are stuck, this book is for you. In 21 Days to Live Life Stronger you will have new habits, knowledge and self-awareness which will empower you to become unstuck and then unstoppable.

This book is comprised of six Growth Zones, each is designed to build on the previous Zone in this book. Growth Zone One looks at building small daily habits and healthy routines. Starting our day with a good routine enables us to set positive intentions and plan for the day ahead; whilst evening routines such as gratitude journals and reflections on what we have done well enable us to foster a positive frame of mind on a daily and ongoing basis.

Growth Zone Two looks at how we understand and manage our emotions. Very often we can feel anxious, stressed, overwhelmed or experience low mood. Most of us, at some time in our lives, will experience emotions we don't understand, and don't know where they have come from. For example, a person who gives greatly to others, may often experience resentment that their help is not appreciated or reciprocated —this person might not understand that it is resentment that they are experiencing, or why it is arising. They experience emotions as 'feeling sad', or 'feeling great discomfort' and often can't quite describe what or how they are feeling.

Growth Zone Three explores the role of our Inner Critic and how we can learn to not let that negative voice influence us. Our Inner Critic is that voice in our head that will be quick enough to tell us we are not doing enough, we are not good enough, we should be doing more, we shouldn't be doing things for ourselves; it essentially puts us down, berates us and is very critical. Very often we say incredibly cruel or hurtful things to ourselves, that we would never dream of saying to another person, but somehow, we accept it for ourselves. In this Growth Zone we will look at strategies to help you understand and, most importantly, silence your Inner Critic.

Growth Zone Four will help you understand and overcome your limiting beliefs. We all have them, and very often we may live our lives without even consciously realising they exist at all. Limiting beliefs are entrenched negative beliefs we hold, for example, 'I will fail/I am a failure' or (one of the most common) 'I am not good enough', or 'people will laugh at me', or 'I'll be rejected', or 'other people's needs are more important than mine'... the list really does go on. These beliefs are not based on fact, or evidence, they are in fact false beliefs, based on early childhood experiences, and they are designed to keep us safe. In this Growth Zone you will learn your most common limiting beliefs and the strategies you can use immediately to help you transform them.

Growth Zone Five is all about understanding our helpful and unhelpful coping strategies. Whilst we may all have an array of helpful coping mechanisms, most of us also have a number of unhelpful coping strategies. These are easy to access at times of stress, anxiety or overwhelm and they have the fastest and biggest impact, for example, comfort eating, use of alcohol, cigarettes, mindless social media use. These strategies help us numb our feelings, avoid uncomfortable thoughts, and temporarily silence the inner critic. Unhelpful coping strategies enable us to put up psychological barriers. But putting up such barriers leads to emotional and psychological distress. In this Growth Zone you will learn to identify your unhelpful coping mechanisms and start to take the right steps to replace them with helpful, positive strategies.

Growth Zone Six looks at the costs of compassion. So many clients that I have worked with are deeply compassionate people. And being compassionate is a wonderful quality. These people willingly give time, energy, empathy, and compassion to those around them, they have a strong desire to 'fix' situations and/or people and they often work in caring roles such as nursing, teaching, mental health and social care. However, in the course of my coaching with such individuals, I have seen first-hand what the personal costs are to deeply compassionate individuals. In this Growth Zone we will explore the uncomfortable emotions and thoughts such as guilt, resentment and anger (emotions that deeply compassionate people don't like to acknowledge) and the connection between compassion and unhelpful coping strategies. Importantly, you will learn techniques to help you set realistic boundaries to protect your wellbeing, whilst still being the compassionate person you are.

Finally, there will be a review of your learning throughout the 21 Days to Live Life Stronger Programme and to consider the changes you want to maintain and develop in the days, weeks and years ahead.

We have but one precious life, this is not a rehearsal and you cannot simply start again if you make mistakes along the way. The tools, techniques and strategies you learn in this book will help you to embrace life with all its imperfections. In short, you will learn how to Live Life Stronger.

Enjoy, as you embark on your journey and adventure.

Further Support

One last thing, I know that many self-development and wellbeing books can only get half way through before we put it to one-side. Particularly when it depends on a daily activity. For this reason I also run an online 21 Day Live Life Stronger Programme, where you will receive short daily videos, support in a private Facebook community and online group calls via Zoom. If you feel you would benefit from this additional support, please follow this link: https://bit.ly/21DaysLLS, or scan the QR code.

GROWTH ZONE 1. BUILDING DAILY HABITS AND HEALTHY ROUTINES

Introduction to Growth Zone One

Having good daily habits and routines provide a foundation to Living Life Stronger. They help us to maintain good health and gives us an anchor so that life's ups and downs are much less likely to derail us.

Healthy habits and routines help us to maintain our emotional health so that we are more able to withstand the everyday stressors that can build up and edge us closer to our 'Stress Threshold'. These means we can tolerate and ignore everyday hassles because we build up an armoury – good daily habits and healthy routines which help us build a protection against life's hassles and daily grind.

When we have positive, healthy habits and routines, we can bounce back more quickly. A good morning routine can ground us and give us a solid foundation; especially if we often 'slip' or 'go off the rails' with our intentions.

Completing a journal in the morning and evening can be a really helpful way to set intentions and maintain helpful habits.

When you read Day 1, you will see the exact journal that I write out on a daily basis. I set my intentions and remind myself of the good habits that help me to stay grounded and set my day up well. Having routines around planning food and a simple plan of my day means I take a lot of thinking time out of my day. And I do this journal and short planning in the morning, over a cup of tea.

I plan good daily habits around exercise, food, rest and connection. The thing I don't mention in my journal but is of equal importance to these daily habits is sleep routines, or more to the point evening routines that lead to good sleep hygiene. I will look at all of these in the first three days of the 21 Days to Live Life Stronger programme.

Before we begin, consider the following questions:

What daily habits do you already have, or want to build into your daily routine? What new activity might work for you?

What evening routines do you currently do, or could you change to help to improve your sleep?

Day 1. Let's Get Started!

The first Growth Zone is Building Daily Habits and Healthy Routines.

We are going to start this 21-day adventure with journalling. There are books written on the power of journalling, how to do it, when to do it, what to write in it. There is so much advice out there that just the idea of starting a journal can feel overwhelming, and so we may never start! Or you may buy an expensive or fancy looking Journal Notebook and only complete the first two or three pages. Not this time, my friend! Today I would like to demystify the notion of journalling. As with so many things, I would urge you to start with a simple way. I'm going to share with you a technique I learnt from one of my mentors, Andy Ramage.

For me, journalling enables me to establish and maintain healthy habits and routines as a daily practice. I am passionate about using journalling to help me establish healthy, positive daily habits and routines for some of the following reasons:

- ✓ Journalling gives me 5-10 minutes in the morning to just focus on me, how I'm feeling, my goals, and my day ahead;
- ✓ Having a positive, healthy routine helps prevent a build-up of stress, and gives me a higher threshold before stress becomes overwhelming;
- ✓ The same daily habits and routines form a solid foundation for when life does throw curveballs, it's a place to 'come back to' which provides certainty and predictability;
- ✓ Having routines saves a massive amount of thinking time on a daily basis;
- ✓ It provides the anchor and the foundation for good emotional wellbeing.

I am aware that for some people, establishing routines feels boring. It takes spontaneity out of your day and feels rigid - like you are a prisoner to a regime. I know why it feels like that, because that is how it used to feel for me! I am by nature an impulsive person; I have to work hard to harness that and find appropriate outlets to unleash my impulsivity! What I have found is that there is order in the daily healthy routine that, in fact, gives me more freedom and more free time to do the other things I want to do.

Some of my clients in the past have started from practically zero, with little routine and certainly no healthy habits. We always start with easy steps, such as 'drink a glass of lemon water' or 'walk for 10 minutes'. The reason we start with easy steps is that you instantly gain a 'win'. Gaining daily wins is really important in maintaining your motivation to keep going (NB, Your 'Chimp' loves it! We will be looking at your Chimp in Growth Zone 2).

A Journal really doesn't have to be complicated. See Figure 1 for how my journal looks. You can see that I create a do-able list of healthy habits that are easily built into the day. You may already have some good habits and that is absolutely great if you have; but what else could you add in? If you are starting from scratch, that is fine too. But start small; start with small achievable steps, so that you accumulate WINS on a daily basis. Creating WINS will also mean that you don't get overwhelmed and give up at the first hurdle. My daily journal also includes mantras, or affirmations, that keep my mindset focused (see Growth Zone 3), by reminding me of the person I want to become as I move towards the best version of me. Some people also use journalling to write about their thoughts and feelings, this is especially effective if you are facing challenges or decisions.

Your task for today is to try out a journal entry. All you need is a piece of paper. Better still a plain lined notebook. That's as fancy as it really 'needs' to be, don't wait until you have bought the perfect notebook! We've all done that, and we all have a shelf full of half-completed notebooks – don't let this lead you to procrastination. In the words of a famous sportswear slogan, Just Do It.

Many people think you have to write and reflect for a long time – this is not necessary, especially at the start of this particular journey. If you are new to journalling, then start with simple steps. I use my journal to write down a particular goal I am working on, for example, finishing this book. Then I write out the steps or activities I need to undertake each day for my day to be a healthy routine, well planned, and that will enable me to get a step closer to my goal.

Figure 1. Example of Journal

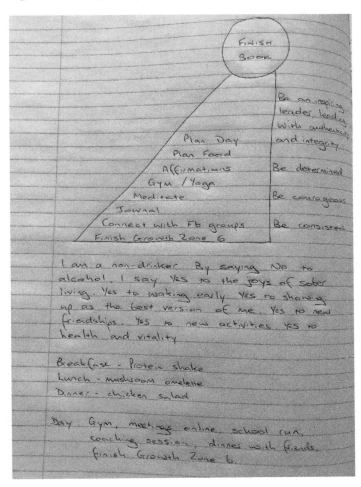

As you will see, my goal is written clearly in the 'moonshot'. Within the triangle, these are the steps needed to reach my goal. For me to reach any goal, I need healthy habits and routines to be in place and allow them to become well established.

So, you will see the following steps:

- ➤ Journal
- ➤ Meditate
- ➤ Yoga stretch/gym
- ➤ Affirmations
- ➤ Plan Day
- ➤ Plan Food
- ➤ Connect with friends/family
- ➤ Write for 30 minutes
- ➤ Complete Growth Zone 6

Reflection Day 1: How does it feel to start writing a journal? What do you think will help you to continue using a journal? What are the potential obstacles?

Day 2. Adding to your healthy daily habits and routines

Yesterday you started writing in a journal to give you the framework to establish your daily habits and routines that will enable you to save time, focus on what's important and keep well. Establishing positive daily habits and routines is incredibly important and that's the reason for it being the first Growth Zone. Today the activity that we will be concentrating on will be to add one more healthy habit to your existing routine.

To get started today, I'd like you to write down any healthy habits or routines you already do; for example, this might be walking your dog in the morning, drinking hot water with lemon to start your day, a ten-minute meditation, and so on. Think carefully about what you already do, that is a healthy habit. Very often we are already doing things that are good for us, and because it is a habit we don't think about it. I would like you to consciously think about these things now. Using the Table below, write down what daily healthy habits you already do.

My Healthy Habits, What I Already Do

My Daily Healthy Habits - things I already do

What I would like you to do now is to think about tiny habits you could start now (or restart if it's something you have previously done). Through this process you're going to identify ONE new (or renewed) habit which you feel you can add into your daily routine, TODAY. But we're going to do this in two steps.

So, you've noted down all the things you already do, and now you feel you can add one more tiny habit to that.

Think of all the things you could add to your list. Perhaps it's walking up and downstairs or doing some squats while the kettle is boiling, or doing 5 press ups before your morning shower. Anything. Be creative. What healthy habit could you add to what you already do. If you are starting completely from scratch, think through a usual day; do you walk at lunchtime, or walk to work. Could you park further from the office to add extra steps or exercise into your day? Could you cycle to work? Could you start eating a piece of fruit after lunch? Could you swap biscuits for houmous and peppers? Write these in the second box.

For now, I would like you to get creative, just think and write down lots of ideas, things you *could* do; not all the things you *must* or *ought* to do.

From this list of possibilities, choose one thing. Just one. And add that to the third box. You can now add this habit to your journal as part of your list of healthy habits you commit to today because they will help you have a great and positive day.

The most important thing is that any intention you set needs to be a small, manageable change, stay away from huge unrealistic goals and targets. Just one small addition to any healthy habits you already have. Write it down, alongside all your existing routines or daily habits. Tomorrow morning, add it in when you are writing your journal.

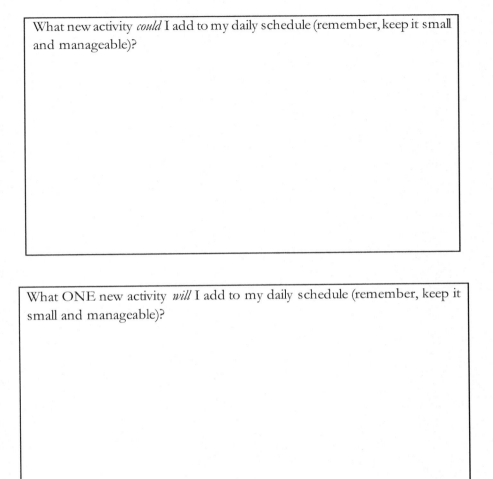

What new activity *could* I add to my daily schedule (remember, keep it small and manageable)?

What ONE new activity *will* I add to my daily schedule (remember, keep it small and manageable)?

Remember to add this when you write in your Journal tomorrow.

Reflection Day 2: What challenges, if any, did you experience in finding one small habit that you could add to your routine? Did you find it easy to be creative and then just choose one thing, or was it difficult to think of new habits to try out?

Day 3. Healthy habits and routines – food planning

One of the reasons I am so keen on establishing healthy daily habits and routines is because it saves so much thinking time and also saves us having to make dozens and dozens of micro-decisions on a daily basis.

A classic example is food planning.

My guess is that in all likelihood you have had a similar experience to this: you're driving home from work, tired and hungry. You need to stop at the supermarket to get something in for dinner. Then you wonder what to have for dinner, mentally going through your fridge at home trying to remember what might be in there or what else you might be running out of. You get into the supermarket and you change your mind over what you thought you might have. You scan the shelves; the item you wanted isn't there. You text your partner "what do you fancy for dinner?" then find yourself browsing things you never even thought about before, still no closer to deciding what to have for dinner. Your partner texts back "Don't mind, you decide", now you're cross because you can't decide either, and why is it always you who has to sort this out anyway… off goes that inner voice! You end up buying something quick and easy and blow all your good intentions for 'the diet' again…

Hopefully, you have also tried food planning, most people give it a go, trying to plan meals over a week, but often we get bored and let it go, and then we spiral back to a similar scenario to the one I have outlined above.

It's taken me a while, but I now do my dinner planning over a 2-week cycle, a week 1 menu and a week 2 menu; and I allow wriggle room so that if we want to have something spontaneous we can. I also plan my food daily and this takes seconds to review (because I have the weekly dinner plan already in place). With my daily plan I include my breakfast and lunch as well as dinner and I keep a list of healthy snacks so I can avoid the temptations of sweets and cakes!

The main reason I do food planning is to avoid the situation above – I am a big fan of reducing our daily micro-decisions, and for me, making decisions about food when I am tired, hungry and just wanting to get home is a terrible time to try to make good decisions.

Good habits, routines and good planning, help us to avoid these bad decisions, and reduce stress that we just don't need to have in our lives.

If you don't currently do food planning, then I really encourage you to give it a try. Use the tools in the Appendix to help you plan your weekly dinners to start with.

In the Appendix you will find some additional tools to help you, including a habit card to record your daily habits and also a food planner. I'm not a dietician, I'm certainly not here to say what you should or shouldn't eat, but planning our food means we don't have to think about it for the rest of the day. And that makes everyday life easier, reduces stress and gives us more free time.

Reflection Day 3: What barriers do you face in planning your food for the week ahead? If a week is too much, then try just planning the weekday meals to begin with. Or even, just three days worth of meals.

Day 4. Don't Aim for Perfection!

At the beginning of this Growth Zone, I outlined why I believe healthy daily habits provide a vital foundation for our wellbeing, including our physical, mental and emotional health.

Having said that, I am now going to say... don't expect to be perfect! Establishing healthy habits shouldn't be an exercise in giving ourselves a long 'to do' list which we *must* achieve every day. Being a slave to a to do list of any kind is not helpful and it doesn't provide the foundation we are seeking for good emotional wellbeing.

What we are trying to establish with journaling and daily habits is a routine that is helpful for you; not another 'task' that sets you up for failure. Often, we need to practice self-compassion around these things. Sometimes we don't do everything we would like to, or intend to. That's ok. Well, it's ok some of the time. The most important thing is to set an intention and to follow that through *most of the time.*

Sometimes life gets really busy; sometimes we are on holiday; or we are away for the weekend and we don't do our journal or daily habits and routines. That's ok. So long as *most of the time* we follow through with the intentions that we set.

Remember, the reason for setting up our day well is to promote our physical, mental and emotional health. We are setting a solid foundation That means not beating ourselves up and allowing the Inner Critic to find its voice (more on this in Growth Zone 3) if sometimes we don't achieve all that we want to.

Set realistic intentions for daily habits and be kind to yourself if on occasion you don't fulfil every intention. Remember, we are looking for progress, *not* perfection.

Reflection Day 4: What progress have you made so far with your daily habits? Are you already striving for perfection? What has been the most useful tool you have used so far in helping you to build positive healthy habits?

Growth Zone 2. Why We Feel the Way We Do - Managing Emotions

Introduction to Growth Zone Two.

In this Growth Zone, we will begin to understand why we feel the way we do. We often get anxious, stressed or overwhelmed; sometimes when we give greatly or unconditionally to others, we can end up feeling resentful and angry towards those who we feel take us for granted, or treat us badly.

Professor Steve Peters is the author of a fantastic book, "The Chimp Paradox", which I use to help clients understand their emotions, their reactions, and their responses. Using the concept of a Chimp to understand our emotions, we are able to understand that our emotional responses are very different to a rational human brain response.

The Chimp Brain is based on fear. The Chimp needs to keep us safe, so is always on the lookout for danger, and can sometimes encourage to react inappropriately or prevent you taking the right action. For example, if you feel anxious about being in social situations, your Chimp Brain will tell you not to go out. However, this doesn't solve the problem, because you still feel anxious, and now your world has become smaller! So we have to understand what triggers our fears, anxiety or stress and we have to be honest about what the root causes are. Usually, because we try to avoid uncomfortable feelings we push away our worries or fears, but this doesn't help to resolve them and it stops us from Living Life Stronger.

If possible, complete the exercises and reflections when you are feeling calm and relaxed, and not when you are in a state of high anxiety or stress.

Day 5. Understanding Why We Feel the Way We Do

The Growth Zone topic for today is **Understanding Why We Feel the Way We Do.**

When we are in a highly emotional state, we are reactive. Cortisol and adrenaline are hormones released by the adrenal glands to indicate that we must be ready for 'fight, flight or freeze' mode. When we experience chronic stress and worry we are constantly in a state of being ready for immediate action. However, our modern-day reaction to this state of readiness is rarely to take immediate physical action, because we are rarely facing physical threats. Instead, most of our worries and stressors are psychological. For example, a person living in a controlling relationship will have extremely high levels of cortisol and adrenaline in their system but will feel helpless to take action to change the situation. So they live continuously with high levels of stress. Similarly, if a person is unhappy in their job but is unable to change jobs due to financial necessity, they will live with high levels of stress (cortisol and adrenaline) but again feel helpless to make changes. Other examples include where we ruminate on the past, berating ourselves for action (or not) that we have taken in the past, or worrying about the future (which by definition hasn't yet happened and so is beyond our control!). When we worry about these high stress situations it is not an action or a behaviour that is affecting us, these worries are just are our thoughts about the past and the future; but just having those thoughts running through our head will produce high levels of stress hormones.

When we have high levels of stress hormones in our system, we are more reactive, we are less rational, we are prone to more physical and psychological illness. So it makes sense to have greater control of our emotions, which will help us to lower the level of stress hormones running through our body and brain which will help up to feel calmer, more at peace and to make decisions rationally, rather than reactively.

The activity for this Growth Zone is to complete a Triggers Worksheet to help you understand the people or situations that trigger you to feel anxious, stressed, angry or simply overwhelmed.

It will be easier to do this when you are feeling relatively calm, and not in a state of high anxiety or stress. I know this isn't always possible, but it is easier to over-ride your Chimp Brain, with your Rational Brain when you are feeling calm.

Use the Triggers and Stressors Worksheet in the Appendix to help you identify the triggers (this might be people, places, memories, etc), write down how you feel emotionally about these triggers, and use the next column to see if you can identify familiar patterns "what typically happens"; these patterns are nearly always there. Then, finally, write down what you would like to have happen. Quite often we want something 'big' to change, or something unrealistic. Try to be realistic about what you want to be different, and then consider the first tiny step to help make the change you want to be a reality.

Reflection Day 5: What was your experience of completing the Triggers Worksheet? Did you experience any resistance to completing the exercise? If so, how did you manage that resistance?

Day 6. Choosing to Respond Rather than React

Very often when we are feeling in a highly emotional state, whether that is feeling anxious, or stressed or simply overwhelmed we tend to be very reactive - reacting emotionally to people or events around us. The clients I work with tend to be deeply compassionate people, who give so much time and energy to others that they can end up feeling resentful and angry towards those who seem to take them for granted, or that feel as though they are being treated badly or without respect.

When I introduced Growth Zone 2, I described the concept of the "Chimp Brain" (and I recommend the book "The Chimp Paradox" by Professor Steve Peters) where we see our emotions and emotional reactions as similar reactions to those you might see in a Chimp. Steve Peters uses the metaphor of a Chimp to explain our emotional brain, and this is a very good way to help us see the difference between our emotional reactions, and our rational human brain response. The two are very different indeed!

The Chimp Brain is reactive and fear-based. It is the most primitive part of our brain and reacts the same as it did when are neanderthal ancestors roamed the earth. Our Chimp brain is always on the lookout for danger, and, if you think about it, through natural evolution, we have inherited genes from those ancestors who successfully kept us alive and safe from threat and danger. So when we feel highly anxious about an argument, an event, being reprimanded by a boss, we can blame our very successful ancestors and their fear-based, reactive brains! That, and natural evolution.

Your Chimp will also seek to make you save energy. We evolved to hunt and gather, to be active humans. As a species we are now largely sedentary (particularly in Western cultures). So, if the alarm goes off early and you had set the intention to get up and go to the gym, your Chimp will be the first to give you feedback that you really would be better off staying in bed. We are often battling a force of nature when we are acting against the 'advice' of our Chimp.

This is why we have to understand what triggers our Chimp brain. What has led to fears, anxiety or stress and what are the root causes. Numbing or trying to ignore uncomfortable feelings doesn't make them go away. It generally leads to more distress and it prevents us from Living Life Stronger.

Using the same Triggers and Stressors Worksheet that you used yesterday, and thinking about what you would like to be different in how things happen, think through the logical steps you might need to take to start making changes happen for the long term.

In order to change our reactions, we first have to raise awareness of our emotions and our behaviours (see Day 5), we then have to choose to do something differently (plan a different response); when we start taking these steps we can start to choose to RESPOND, rather than REACT.

And when we respond, we are living in a calmer state (most of the time) - we are better able to consider our responses to any situation and we are better able to consider other people's perspectives. This makes us more rational human beings, and enables us to make decisions thoughtfully, rather than reacting inappropriately.

Reflection Day 6: How easy was it to think about different outcomes once you had raised your awareness of what your triggers are? Are the actions realistic that you have considered?

Day 7. Managing Our Chimp, Part 1

In this Growth Zone we are using the metaphor of a Chimp to help us understand the very impulsive, fearful emotional brain that we have, that exists alongside our human rational brain. When we are in Chimp Mode we react, we are more anxious, stressed or overwhelmed; we say things we don't mean, to the wrong people, at the wrong time. In a word, we are *reactive*.

It is very important then that we understand how to manage our Chimp. As Steve Peters shows, there are 3 steps to managing our Chimp:

First, Exercise the Chimp;

Second, Box the Chimp;

Third. Feed it Bananas.

To exercise the Chimp, we must first let off steam! Basically, talk it out, get all the negative energy out - but we must do this with the right person. Often, we turn to the nearest person, or a partner or close friend, and this might not always be the right person. When choosing who to help us exercise our chimp we need someone who:

(1) will listen without judgement;

(2) won't interrupt, except to seek clarification;

(3) (and this is perhaps the most important bit) won't try to solve the problem or issue.

When you're Chimp has used up all its negative energy (and we all know how it feels to "get it off your chest") then we are ready to 'Box the Chimp'

In the second stage of Chimp Management, we are able to rationally explore the possible solutions to the problem or trigger that is creating the emotional reaction in us. When we have released the negative energy in Step 1 of Chimp Management, we are better able to say to our Chimp "now you are calm, listen to these possible solutions, trust me (the adult, rational human), I've got this".

Objectifying our emotional brain, or our Chimp, in this way can be really helpful in stopping us reacting, and instead choosing how we respond. When our Chimp is calm, our emotions are calm, and then we are much better able to think logically and rationally.

Your task today is to identify a 'Chimp Buddy', a trusted confidante to whom you can vent your emotional reactions, who won't judge you, who will allow you free rein to say things in complete confidence and (importantly) who won't try to fix the problem for you. Personally, I have a very good friend who is an incredibly busy person, but we can each send a text when necessary saying "my Chimp needs a friend". That message then means that at the earliest opportunity we will ring back and listen (having a shared understanding of the Chimp is quite handy, because you know the matter is urgent, but that all you need to do is listen).

Reflection Day 7: To what extent can you identify with the steps of Chimp Management? What is your experience of 'exercising the Chimp' (venting!) to the wrong person at the wrong time? Consider how this experience would improve if you followed the 3 steps of Chimp Management.

Day 8. Managing Our Chimp, Part 2

Yesterday I said how important it is to manage our chimp, and outlined the first 2 steps. Today we are going to focus on the third and final step. The third step is to Feed the Chimp Bananas.

Today we will look at how to get our Chimp on our side. How do we get this reactive brain to work with us? Quite often our Chimp will derail our very best intentions. For example, perhaps you have an early start? The alarm goes off at 5.30am - chances are your Chimp wants to stay in bed! Do you find procrastination is a problem? That's your Chimp! Do you find you self-sabotage? Again... that's your Chimp in charge. So often we are at the whim of our emotions. How we feel dictates what we do; and this can lead to overwhelm, stress, procrastination and a sense of failure when we don't get the things done that we know need to be completed.

So, we need ways to get our Chimp to work with us, rather than against us. There are two main ways to do this and both come under the phrase "Feeding the Chimp Bananas". If you think of our Chimp as being like a small child, they love praise and reward; they can also be (relatively) easily distracted. *Reward* and *Distraction* are two ways to feed your Chimp bananas. In the first case we can reward our Chimp if it helps us. For example, let's say you want to set an intention to get up 30 minutes earlier to do an exercise routine; left to its own devices your Chimp will make every excuse not to get out of bed earlier; however, if we set up a 'reward', e.g., meet a friend at the gym; coffee straight after; a note to an accountability group etc, then your Chimp is much more likely to be on board with the activity as it is focussed on the reward, not the (perceived painful) activity.

Similarly, we can use *distraction* as an effective way of managing our Chimp. Using the same example, we would set our gym clothes out the night before, then when the alarm goes off we say to the Chimp "5, 4, 3, 2, 1, out of bed" there is no time for arguments to be raised, we must launch straight to action - before the Chimp has time to start arguing, we are already out of bed and dressed. By now it is much harder for the Chimp to argue that we should stay in bed.

We can use the same kind of techniques when we are procrastinating. For example, if we have 100 emails to get through, our Chimp has switched off before we start, and is making excuses as to why it's an impossible task. In this case we can negotiate with our Chimp, for example, we might say "if we get the first 5 done, then we can stop for a coffee", chances are, once you get started, you'll be able to continue without too much trouble. Often getting started is the biggest hurdle.

Reflection Day 8: Write down times when your Chimp usually takes control. What kinds of tasks, or events, are undermined by your Chimp taking over? What rewards or distractions could you initiate so that you regain control over your Chimp?

GROWTH ZONE 3. SILENCING THE INNER CRITIC

Introduction to Growth Zone Three.

In Growth Zone 3 we explore our Inner Critic. The Inner Critic is something everyone experiences from time to time, and for some people it is something they experience almost all of the time. The Inner Critic is that voice in our head that is judging us and watching over our every thought and action. The Inner Critic will be quick enough to tell us we are not doing enough, we are not good enough, we should be doing more, telling us we are selfish if we put our needs above others - essentially putting us down, berating us and being very critical.

The Inner Critic shows up as a result of early childhood experiences, and although we are now adults we are believing, thinking and behaving in ways that are shaped by the rules, values and actions of caregivers around us when we were young. So, if you were parented in a way that expected very high standards of academic achievement, then you might well recognise be a perfectionist. Another way to look at this is that you have a strong Inner Critic voice that says "I'm not good enough".

We often try to **not** listen to this voice (because, let's face it, it isn't very nice!); however, if we listen in, understand where it is coming from and what it is saying, we can start to challenge it with compassion. The chances are you wouldn't dream of speaking to others the way you speak to yourself. Therefore, think: "would I speak to my best friend this way?" If the answer is no, then you probably need to work on changing how you speak to yourself.

The Worksheet that accompanies this Growth Zone will help you to identify the Inner Critic, what is it saying, and when; then you can start practising what you would say to quieten it down.

Day 9. Understanding Our Inner Critic

Day 9 and we begin to understand our Inner Critic. Where does that voice in our head come from? Why is it there? Why is it *so* cruel? The very short answer to those questions comes down to our values, beliefs, and our upbringing. However, it is not a simple explanation.

It is hard to believe that our Inner Critic has a useful purpose when it can be incredibly cruel and put us down constantly. So many people tell themselves (through their Inner Critic) that they are not good enough, not clever enough, not funny enough, that people don't like them, that they are pathetic, that no-one will ever love them, and so on.

In order to start to understand our Inner Critic, we must first listen and pay attention to what is being said. This can be difficult and emotionally challenging, but this is a much needed first step in the process of learning to silence your Inner Critic.

When we learn to silence our Inner Critic, we build our confidence and self-esteem. We push our own limits and boundaries, and we can start to believe in ourselves again.

The exercise today, that accompanies this Growth Zone is the Inner Critic Worksheet, which you will find in the Appendix.

When you start raising your own awareness of your Inner Critic, and writing and journalling about it, you will begin to see patterns emerging about what it says, and under what circumstances. This exercise isn't something only to do once, but something you should repeat on a regular basis until you start to recognise the underlying patterns.

In the Worksheet, you will see some examples of where the Inner Critic might show up. For example, you might find that you don't ever put yourself forward for a job promotion because the Inner Critic might say things like: *"You know you won't be able to do the job. Who do you think you are, thinking you are good enough for that role? Why are you even trying? You know you are not good enough. There are other people much better than you who will apply. Seriously, who do you think you are?!"*

In today's exercise it would be helpful to write down the situations where your Inner Critic shows up. For me, mine used to show up a lot when I was going through my divorce, many years ago now. The voice would tell me I was such a rubbish mum, that I was ruining my children's lives by leaving their dad, that I was hurting them because I couldn't give them the lifestyle they would have if I stayed with their dad. It would go on relentlessly, yada, yada, yada... and would mock me when I became upset, telling me I was pathetic and look - here was proof of what a terrible mum I was.

The reason my Inner Critic was so loud and so critical is because leaving my marriage was against my core values of family; it also challenged the beliefs I had grown up with from a young age, that parents *should* stay together 'for the sake of the family'. Admittedly, this is quite an outdated idea now, but you have to remember that for my parents' generation, divorce was mostly unthinkable in any circumstance.

The Inner Critic is formed from our experiences of early childhood. It often reflects the values and beliefs of our caregivers and how we were parented. When we were children, we took on these 'rules', values and beliefs and often behaved in ways that complied with our caregivers wishes. As adults we continue some of those patterns, but they are much less helpful to us as autonomous adults instead of children. The purpose of our Inner Critic is to try to prevent us breaking those rules or patterns from early childhood.

There will be many areas of your life where the Inner Critic might show up. Professionally, when you are alone, and also within our family and friendship groups. Use the prompts in the Inner Critic Worksheet to explore exactly where and when your Inner Critic shows up; and start to consider where these criticisms originated.

Reflection Day 9: In what area of your life does your Inner Critic show up the most? Are there parts of your life, say your professional life, which is untouched by your Inner Critic, whilst others, for example., your parenting skills, where your Inner Critic is loud. Why do you think these differences exist?

Day 10. Using Compassion to Silence Our Inner Critic

Today we will continue with Growth Zone 3, which is all about Silencing the Inner Critic.

As we saw yesterday, our Inner Critic can be malicious and unkind. We often try to **not** listen to this voice (because, let's face it, it isn't very nice!); and we might try to use unhelpful coping strategies to shut out the noise. I'll come back to this tomorrow.

However, if we raise our awareness of our Inner Critic we can begin to replace the unkind, critical words with kind, compassionate words instead. As a rule, if you find yourself speaking to yourself in a way that you would never speak to a good friend, then you need to moderate the way you are allowing the Inner Critic to speak to you. You do have the ability to change the dialogue and then start speaking to yourself the say way you would to a good friend.

Self-compassion is one of the most powerful tools in our psychological armoury to protect ourselves from the deep criticism from the Inner Critic. Speaking to ourselves as kindly as we would to a good friend, is a great start to quietening down the voice of the Inner Critic. Using the same example as yesterday, if a friend were thinking of going for a job promotion, I'm sure you wouldn't tell them they are ridiculous for even thinking they might be able to apply. What would you say instead? Perhaps you would encourage them to read the advert or request more information; or to think about their skills and how that might fit with the job. Or even, a simple "go for it, what have you got to lose? I believe in you".

Going back to the Worksheet you started yesterday, where you have written what the Inner Critic typically says to you, I want you to now write down what you would say to a good friend in the same circumstances.

Now apply those same words and sentiments to yourself.

You can start creating new scripts and ways of speaking to yourself with kindness, to quieten down the tone and volume of your Inner Critic.

Another example you might consider is this: instead of "I should have achieved more and finished all that work", you could reframe this by saying to yourself "I have done the very best I can with the time and resources I have, I would not expect more of anyone else, so I will accept my best is more than good enough".

It is worth writing these scripts down in your journal. I have done this with clients, where they have created scripts and repeat them in a mantra several times a day. This strategy can work extremely well, but it does take practice and repetition. Remember, you have a lifetime of the Inner Critic's negativity to overcome, it won't happen in a single day!

Reflection Day 10: How does it feel to treat yourself with Self-Compassion? If it is uncomfortable, try simply sitting with that discomfort. If you meditate, try meditating, or use mindfulness to gently accept your gift to yourself of self-compassion.

Day 11. Numbing or Avoiding Our Inner Critic

The Growth Zone topic today concerns how we try to avoid, ignore or numb that critical voice in our head. Our Inner Critic is a huge source of negativity for us. Did you know we have around 70,000 thoughts a day, and for many people 80% of those thoughts are negative? As if that's not bad enough, negative thoughts are 6-7 times more powerful than positive ones. That's a whole lot of negativity we are carrying around and listening to in our head!

We often try to ignore that voice or block it out with numbing behaviours like comfort eating, perfectionism, using alcohol, or online shopping to make us feel better in the moment. Such behaviours may help us to side-step the Inner Critic in the moment, but it really only offers a brief respite. Avoidant or numbing behaviours can actually make things worse because it gives our Inner Critic more ammunition than it originally had. Often our avoidant or numbing behaviours have a detrimental impact on our health (for example, consider the impact of daily drinking on long term health), they are also often in conflict with our own values (for example, wanting to live a healthy lifestyle) which then enables our Inner Critic to start up "what about that diet?", "you said you wouldn't drink tonight" and on and on it goes. Relentless. We will be looking more at unhelpful coping strategies in Growth Zone 5.

The other thing we may do is not try to overcome the Inner Critic at all, instead, staying small and never trying to do more, be more or achieve more. We may do nothing at all, and in doing so we ensure we can't be criticised for failing, but we also can't be praised for achieving or for following our purpose.

Having a sense of purpose, a sense that you are fulfilling what you were put on this planet to achieve, is an important aspect of psychological wellbeing. Settling for staying in your comfort zone will usually lead to a sense of dissatisfaction, disharmony. and unhappiness.

The reflection for today is to go back to your Worksheet and consider whether you use any avoidant or numbing behaviours to try to shut out your Inner Critic. When might this happen? What are the consequences of your avoidant or numbing behaviours? Write these down in your journal. What would you like to have happen instead of these behaviours?

Reflection Day 11: To what extent do you use any avoidant or numbing behaviours to try to shut out your Inner Critic. When might this happen? What are the consequences of your avoidant or numbing behaviours? What would you like to have happen instead of these behaviours?

GROWTH ZONE 4. WHAT'S HOLDING YOU BACK? LIMITING BELIEFS

Introduction to Growth Zone Four.

"The only thing that's keeping you from getting what you want is the story you keep telling yourself." Tony Robbins.

A limiting belief is an entrenched negative belief, or conviction, that you think to be true and which restricts or limits you in some way. Limiting beliefs can be about you, or how others see you, or about your wider world and place within it. Examples of common limiting beliefs include: "I will fail/I am a failure"; "I am not good enough"; "People will laugh at me"; "I'll be rejected"; "Other's people's needs are more important than mine"; "Other people can't be trusted/will always let you down"... the list really does go on and on. These false beliefs are, more often than not, stored in our subconscious until such time as they are brought into our conscious awareness, either through our own self-development, or from others pointing out the false narrative.

Limiting beliefs can have a negative impact in several ways. Limiting beliefs will stop you seeking and taking new opportunities, they can prevent you making good decisions, and they certainly stop you reaching your full potential. Ultimately, limiting beliefs can keep you stuck in a negative state of mind and get in the way of you living the life you truly desire.

When we hold these false beliefs, we continually retell a story about ourselves, for example, "I am not good enough to go for that job", or "nothing I ever do is good enough for my parents" and so on. Until we seek evidence to the contrary we will continue to retell, and consequently reinforce, this negative belief. But because this belief is an unconscious belief, we never purposefully seek contradictory evidence to test it; until, as I say, the negative belief is brought into conscious awareness.

Thankfully, we don't have to continue to live by these 'stories' that we tell ourselves. We can change them. But it takes small steps and it takes time... But let's make a start!

The purpose of this Growth Zone is to help you begin to bring your unconscious limiting beliefs into your conscious awareness. It is only when we become aware of our limiting beliefs that we can start to take positive action to change them. And when we do that, we open up an exciting world of new opportunities and potential.

Day 12. Identifying Limiting Beliefs

Welcome to Day 12 of the 21 Days to Live Life Stronger book. We are now making good progress on raising your self-awareness and understanding some of your unconscious biases which are keeping you from your full potential.

Today you will complete an exercise that will help you to identify your limiting beliefs. Before we can start to change limiting beliefs, we have to bring them into our conscious awareness.

The activity for today is to complete a worksheet which will help you to identify your main limiting beliefs. Core limiting beliefs tend to be "I'm not good enough"; "I will fail"; "I'll be judged/rejected"; "I'm not worthy/lovable"; "I don't deserve ...xyz"; "Other people's needs are more important than mine"; and "You can't trust anyone". You can see that the Inner Critic (from Growth Zone 3) will jump on these limiting beliefs and reinforce them - that's how they stay entrenched and keep us in our so-called "comfort zone" (often a very uncomfortable and unhappy 'comfort zone').

Limiting beliefs usually come to light when there is something we want to be, or do, or achieve, but then we unconsciously put blocks in our own way. For example, you might secretly want to return to university to study for a degree. Then the narrative will start "I didn't get A levels, I won't be able to study at university", "No-one in my family has been to University, who do I think I am?", "I know I won't be able to do that, so there's no point even trying" and so on. And before long, that secret desire is tucked away in a metaphorical box never to be properly opened and explored. That secret desire then becomes a future regret – one day when you look back at your life, you will see all the opportunities you could have explored and experienced, but didn't. Simply because your limiting beliefs held you back.

Today and tomorrow, we will use the worksheet to start to bring your limiting beliefs into conscious awareness. First you will identify the things you wish you had done, or want to do. Perhaps you want to progress your career, but have never tried to go for promotion; or you want to improve your financial position but believe you can't because you are "bad with money". Or maybe you want to buy your own home, but think it will never be possible. Or maybe you want to travel on your own, but think you are "not allowed" because of the views and opinions of other people. Take time to think about different areas of your life and your aspirations. Then consider carefully and honestly… what is stopping you?

Reflection Day 12: What came to mind when you thought deeply about the things you secretly aspire to be, do or achieve? Imagine you are at the end of your life, looking back at your past, what do you think would be your biggest regret? What steps would you want to take to make sure that regret doesn't happen?

Day 13. Don't Let Limiting Beliefs Hold You Back

Welcome to Day 13 of the 21 Days to Live Life Stronger Programme where we dig a bit deeper into Limiting Beliefs. I'd like to start with a quote that has shaped my life since I started my own transformation after leaving an emotionally abusive marriage.

"The only thing that's keeping you from getting what you want is the story you keep telling yourself." Tony Robbins.

The reason this quote has had such an impact on me is because I held a victim story for a very long time. I'm going to come back to this in Growth Zone 6 where we look at the Costs of Compassion; but in the meantime, it's important to understand that our own beliefs, which we often hold sub-consciously, can really hold us back.

Limiting beliefs come from early childhood experiences; the way we were parented, the way our educators treated us and the environment we grew up in. If you went to a school where your creative work was scorned or discouraged, it is unlikely that you will be artistic or creative in adulthood. If your parents had unrealistic expectations of you as a child, then you may well be a perfectionist. The positive and negative consequences of our early childhood impact our subconscious and this impacts our conscious behaviour and decision making.

Have a think about your own early childhood experiences. Were there times that you just wanted your parents to be proud of you? Was love conditional on 'being a good girl'? Were you told "boys don't cry". I am not suggesting that our parents have done anything wrong. Parenting in the 1960s and 1970s was different to how it mostly is today. Our parents had grown up in a harsh post-war era and wanted a better life for their children. The traditional gender roles were still very pervasive, and this shaped the parenting skills of that generation. Every generations' parenting style is shaped by the context they grew up in, the parenting they experienced, and current cultural views. For example, in recent years many parents are identified as "helicopter parents" meaning they are over-protective, pay excessive attention to their children, and are highly involved, not allowing their children to learn from their own mistakes which results in a lack of confidence and self-belief in their children. This is likely to come from this generation's reaction and response to their own experiences as a child, the current environment and increased awareness of safety dangers and the current cultural climate that suggests we need to actively support child development.

Take time to think back and look at your limiting beliefs, I can almost guarantee they are based somewhere within your early experiences.

Reflection Day 13: What feelings came up for you when you considered the impact of your early childhood on your beliefs in adulthood? To what extent could you see a link between your early childhood experiences and your limiting beliefs today?

Day 14. Transforming Limiting Beliefs

Welcome to Day 14 of the 21 Days to Live Life Stronger book. In this Growth Zone we are exploring how to identify limiting beliefs, how they hold us back, and where they originated from. Today we will look at transforming limiting beliefs into positive, *empowering* beliefs.

There are many different strategies that we can use to help us overcome limiting beliefs and I'm going to outline an easy 4 step process here:

Step 1: Ask yourself "Is this a helpful belief" (for example, if you often feel like you are not good enough (in any area of your life), you might hold the belief "other people are better than I am". Is this helpful, or unhelpful, to believe this?

Step 2: Look for contradictory evidence. Write down times when you have been successful, or done something well; this could be literally anything. The closer this evidence is to your limiting belief, the better. For example, you might believe "I am not good enough to apply for a higher paid job". Think of examples where you have been good enough and where have you done well in your work. What compliments have other people paid you? What are your strengths? Where and when have you 'gone the extra mile'? Ask your boss or colleagues for feedback about your work performance. Ask a trusted friend or colleague their opinion about your suitability to apply for a higher paid role.

Step 3: Replace the limiting belief with a new positively focussed belief. Given the successes you identified in Step 2, your new belief could be "I have been successful in my current job"; "Colleagues have commented positively on my impact in the workplace"; "I have many strengths that would make me perfect for the next job" and so on.

Step 4: Create affirmations to reinforce the belief, and write them down daily. For example, you might use an affirmation such as "I am equal to others and what they think of me is out of my control".

There are many other strategies that we can add to our toolkit to transform limiting beliefs and get the inner critic on our side. In my 3 Month Live Life Stronger Programme we spend several sessions looking at these in detail; this

4-step strategy will be enough to get you going for now!

Reflection Day 14: What thoughts came up for you when you considered whether your beliefs are helpful or not? Try spending more time searching for evidence which contradicts your beliefs; be prepared to think more deeply about your limiting beliefs and the contradictory evidence which will almost certainly exist.

The Importance of Self Compassion

Self compassion is a way of thinking about self-care which is vital when we are exploring our psychological wellbeing. Very often when we start exploring below the surface and bringing into conscious awareness the very things we have tried to bury in our mind, we can experience distress, a lack of self-belief and a lack of self-confidence.

This is why I have included the section here on Self compassion. It is not a Growth Zone in and of itself, but it is an important framework which underpins much of the work you are doing in this book.

Day 15. Introducing Self Compassion

Completing the exercises on your emotions and limiting beliefs is likely to have been uncomfortable at times. When we raise awareness of difficult emotions or we see how we have been held back by false beliefs, it can lead to a lower sense of self-worth, or a feeling that we have wasted our time by being kept small in our comfort zone.

Experiencing challenging thoughts and emotions is incredibly common when we do what is known in coaching circles as "deep work". That is why self compassion is so important.

Being kind to ourselves when we are feeling vulnerable makes a big difference to how quickly and how well we process the challenging thoughts or emotions.

Because limiting beliefs and our Inner Critic are very much formed as a result of our early childhood experiences, some people choose to spend time nurturing their Inner Child. To do this, we need to spend time thinking about ourselves from our earliest memories. We can nurture our Inner Child by imagining we are sitting with that child (our younger self), reassuring them and telling them that you are protecting them now. This Inner Child work can be very complex, and if this is something you would like to explore then there are experts such as Marissa Peer (see Resources Section at the end of this book) who provide more information on this subject.

For many people, nurturing their Inner Child can be as simple as having a photograph of yourself as a child, and telling your younger self that you are loved and cared for. That *you* love and care about yourself, and that you love and care for your younger self. If we experienced conditional love, abandonment, or neglect as a child, it is often difficult to express self-love and self compassion, so small steps towards nurturing oneself can have a profound impact.

Being self compassionate is not a passive thought or belief, it requires positive action. There are a number of techniques we can use to transform how we view ourselves and to develop our self-belief and confidence. Two useful techniques you can try are:

1) Identifying our strengths and positive attributes; and
2) Affirmations.

The task for today is to try either, or both, of these techniques.

The first is as simple as writing in your journal and giving yourself time, perhaps 30 minutes or so, to think about and write down your strengths and positive attributes. You can even ask people close to you to help you identify these if you are struggling. For so many of the people I work with, their core strengths tend to be compassion, kindness and empathy. Perhaps you have overcome considerable adversity and you can see how your strengths have developed as a result. Or maybe your friends or peers comment on particular qualities you have. Write these in your journal so you can come back to it and add to your list as time goes on.

The second technique is to create affirmations. For example, Marissa Peer advocates writing on a mirror "I am enough". I write in my journal each day, and my personal affirmations tend to be "I am courageous", "I am determined", "I am loved". It is worth spending some time thinking about affirmations that are personal and right for you. One of my clients had a great deal of self-doubt and self-criticism around her parenting skills, and so she created an affirmation directed solely at her parenting skills.

Where we have an area of our life where we experience a great deal of self-doubt, where our Inner Critic shows up, or where limiting beliefs are obvious, then this is where we need to direct conscious effort in challenging that negative bias with positive re-framing. Finding contrary evidence to our negative thoughts and beliefs as well as identifying strengths and creating positive affirmations are all powerful techniques in reducing our negative patterns and doing so with a great deal of self compassion.

Reflection Day 15: To what extent did you experience any resistance in thinking about yourself in a positive way? What does the concept of 'self compassion' mean for you?

GROWTH ZONE 5. HELPFUL AND UNHELPFUL COPING STRATEGIES

Introduction to Growth Zone Five.

In previous Growth Zones, we have seen how raising awareness of difficult emotions and thoughts can be very uncomfortable. However, this awareness-raising is vital if we want to improve our psychological and emotional wellbeing. Without that, we are carrying around an unconscious burden which can feel overwhelming. Although this burden, or discomfort, is largely unconscious we will still experience distress, even if we are not able to fully explain why – mostly because we want to avoid thinking about it too much, because it is painful. And humans like to avoid pain as much as possible.

This is where unhelpful coping strategies manifest. They are easy to access at times of stress, anxiety or overwhelm and they have the fastest and biggest impact. They help us numb our feelings, avoid thoughts, shut down the Inner Critic and enable us to put up psychological barriers. Neurologically, unhelpful coping mechanisms usually result in an upsurge of dopamine which makes us feel good. This dual effect of numbing discomfort and making us feel better is a powerful combination which makes it very difficult to change these behaviours.

Unhelpful strategies are unhelpful because they don't provide us with resources or capability to resolve the problem, they also fail to help up process difficult emotions and thoughts. They can also lead to addiction and/or dependency issues. Common unhelpful strategies include but are not limited to overuse of food (or over-control of food), alcohol, cigarettes, gaming, gambling, sex, drugs (prescription and illegal) and self-harm. These unskilful strategies contribute to greater mental health issues such as anxiety and stress and reduce our resilience.

On the other side of the coin, helpful positive strategies can help increase our stress threshold, meaning we can deal with more of the problems that life throws at us without becoming overwhelmed. We can use helpful coping strategies in two ways; as a preventative means against stress, or as a response to stress. The better we are at daily positive habits, the better our prevention measures are and then we manage our stress, anxiety or overwhelm more successfully.

Day 16. Helpful, and Unhelpful, Coping Strategies

Welcome to Day 16 of the 21 Days to Live Life Stronger Programme. We are going to start this Growth Zone with unhelpful coping strategies because they are easiest to access at times of stress, anxiety or overwhelm and they have the fastest and biggest impact. However, they are also detrimental to our long-term emotional wellbeing, and some can be damaging to our physical health too.

Unhelpful coping strategies arise as a way of coping with difficult circumstances. Most people have had experiences which are difficult to live with, some of us have to face these on a daily basis. This might be because we have suffered a trauma of some kind, or we have to work in a job that we hate, or we are faced with ongoing financial stress, we have challenging relationships, and so on. Chronic stress is experienced when we see no way of escaping the situation, or cannot think of any solutions to make things better.

Under such difficult circumstances we often try to cope in self-defeating ways. For example, drinking alcohol can help in the moment to relax, to numb emotions, or to shut intrusive thoughts out. However, as an addictive substance alcohol can lead the person to become dependent without them even realising, until they try to cut down or stop and find they cannot. This is an example of a coping strategy which has tipped the balance from being helpful into becoming a negative coping strategy. Another common example is comfort eating. People who are experiencing chronic stress, or a traumatic experience may find themselves eating to feel better, very often the foods of choice will be starchy carbohydrates such as bread, cakes, biscuits and so on. All of which will lead to weight gain if not eaten in moderation.

Negative coping strategies result in negative patterns, we repeat the behaviour even if the source of the problem or stress no longer exists, which in turn lead to negative outcomes. The use of unhelpful coping strategies also prevents the individual from finding and practising positive coping strategies. Hence a downward cycle ensues, and the unhelpful strategies are maintained.

The purpose of the exercise today is to help you identify any unhelpful coping strategies you might use. For this exercise you do not necessarily need to uncover the source of the stress or trauma. For some people this will only be appropriate to do with a trained professional. But instead, just try to identify any unhelpful coping strategies you might use and list them in the worksheet in the Appendix, or in your journal.

The kinds of behaviours are those that you use when you are feeling stressed or overwhelmed, and that make you feel better in the moment (even if you almost instantly regret it). For example, comfort eating, use of alcohol, cigarettes, drugs (of any kind), mindless scrolling on social media, and so on.

At this stage we are only seeking to understand what your unhelpful coping strategies are, and what purpose they serve.

Reflection Day 16: How did you find the exercise today? Was it is easy to identify these unhelpful coping strategies? Did you find it easy or difficult to think about the purpose of the coping strategies (e.g., could you see that you might use unhelpful strategies to numb painful emotions)?

If you have experienced any difficulties in completing this exercise, please go back to Day 15 and practice self compassion. You can also look ahead to Day 17 for positive coping and self care strategies.

Day 17. Helpful Strategies Increase Resilience

Welcome to Day 17 of 21 Days to Live Life Stronger. Today we will look at how helpful coping strategies increase our resilience.

Remember how we built positive daily habits in Growth Zone 1? In a similar way, helpful positive strategies can help increase our stress threshold, meaning we can deal with more of the problems that life throws at us without becoming overwhelmed. We can use helpful coping strategies in two ways, as a preventative means against stress, or as a response to stress. The better we are at daily positive habits, the better our prevention measures will be and, consequently, the better we become at managing our stress, anxiety or overwhelm.

Positive helpful strategies might include exercise, yoga, walking, meditation, reading a book, talking with a friend, having a relaxing bath, having a massage or even a spa day, or perhaps a swim in the sea. When we prioritise self-care and positive coping strategies we are building an insurance policy for ourselves and our emotional wellbeing. This goes back to what we covered in Growth Zone One. When we build healthy positive habits into routines, we are less likely to forget to practice them, and we begin to learn to prioritise our own wellbeing.

When we consciously prioritise our psychological wellbeing, we can start to tackle our unhelpful coping strategies. When our psychological wellbeing is taken care of on an ongoing basis, then we are better able to see why we employ unhelpful coping strategies. So, for example, we might use alcohol as a means of numbing emotions through a traumatic divorce, but once the trauma has passed and we begin to prioritise our psychological health we are likely to rely less on alcohol because we are better placed to manage our emotions.

The downside of this, is that we might realise we have dependency issues which then need to be tackled, but this is beyond the scope of this book (I would advise seeking support from your GP in the first instance, or finding a support group for the problem which you may have now realised is impacting your life).

When we prioritise our own wellbeing, we are much better placed to help others, as well as feeling happier and healthier ourselves. This provides us with a strong foundation to tackle the stresses of life, feel as though we have purpose and generally feel more fulfilled.

Using the same Worksheet as yesterday, please write down which helpful coping strategies you use, and how you might set them up as daily habits.

Reflection Day 17: How did you feel when considering the positive coping strategies you already use? Was it easy to identify these helpful coping strategies?

Day 18. Transforming Unhelpful Strategies

In this Growth Zone 5 we have looked at helpful and unhelpful copies strategies, and you may recall I mentioned that unhelpful coping strategies are those that give us a quick fix because they trigger the dopamine reward system in the brain. Because of this, they are difficult to change, and if we rely solely on willpower then we are likely to struggle to succeed.

Where an unhelpful strategy has become a habitual destructive pattern, then it becomes necessary to create a sustained plan to transform these unhelpful habits.

Transforming unhelpful coping strategies could be a whole book all of its own, but today I would like to invite you to try the following steps if you are struggling to overcome an unhelpful coping strategy (you will have done some of these already in the worksheet). Use the worksheet, or your journal to follow these steps for transformation:

1.Recognise and acknowledge the unhelpful habit/behaviour
- What unhelpful habits or behaviours do you use?
- When does it/they happen?
- Are you numbing your thoughts or emotions (or is this a legacy habit that's become an addictive behaviour?)

2.If you are numbing or avoiding emotions or thoughts, then calmly think about what is going on, and write it down in your journal (refer back to the exercise you did in Growth Zone 2);
- When do those emotions or thoughts arise?
- Do you know why they arise?
- Numbing, avoiding or blocking thoughts and emotions doesn't work, they need to be processed.

3.Write down your 'why'
- Has this behaviour become a problem for you?
- Why do you want to change this behaviour? Some people want to change a behaviour for health reasons or to set a good example to their children.
- What is YOUR reason for wanting change?

4.When you are in a relatively calm state, think about other solutions that could help you avoid the need for the unhelpful coping mechanism

- What helpful and skilful coping strategies could you use instead?
- Consider strategies such as mindfulness, walking, listening to music.
- How could you change your state in the moment, for example, cold water swims/dips/ showers; listening to upbeat music; writing in your journal; phoning a friend, writing affirmations, and so on.

5.Surf the Urge

- If you have an entrenched behaviour, you are likely to experience cravings.
- These can be overwhelming, but, they can be overcome.
- Try meditation, or mindfulness to help calm your mind.
- Cravings typically feel like waves building up, watch with curiosity.
- Try to avoid just giving in to the craving, but acknowledge its existence.

6.Be kind to yourself

- If you 'fall off the wagon', don't worry, look again at your 'why'.
- Listen to a self-compassion guided meditation (there are plenty on YouTube and apps, e.g., Calm, or Insight Timer).
- If you're counting how many days you're avoiding the behaviour don't start on 'Day 1' again; instead, just put the day down to experience, continue your progress tomorrow.
- Look at alternative coping strategies; build new daily habits, get support from friends, or online groups (you can join my free Facebook Community: https://www.facebook.com/groups/livelifestronger).

7.Build daily habits

- Create your 'space', or lifestyle, so that it is difficult for the unhelpful habit to show up (this is a long-term strategy that needs constant nurturing, which is why when I run my 21-day programmes I start with building Healthy Daily Habits).
- For example, if you exercise in the morning, then the desire to do this could be another reason to not drink the night before. Or perhaps you want to try Time Restricted Eating, so you can't eat after 8pm (regardless of whether it is 'comfort food' or not).

I hope these steps have been helpful in identifying and transforming unhelpful habits. They will provide you with another tool in your toolkit, and this will be far more successful than willpower alone. Remember that any kind of transformation of habits takes time and commitment, perseverance is key. You are aiming for progress, not perfection.

Reflection Day 18: Which of the steps was most helpful for you? On a scale of 0-10, how confident are you that you can transform an unhelpful strategy? What would need to happen to increase that confidence level by 1 point?

GROWTH ZONE 6. THE COSTS OF COMPASSION

Introduction to Growth Zone Six

Being compassionate is a wonderful quality. Many compassionate people are very happy, and they make others around them very happy too. I have made it my mission to work with deeply compassionate people. For the clients I work with, compassion is part of who they are; and one of their top values. However, I firmly believe that we need to be honest with ourselves about what compassion *costs* us. Because compassion *can and does* come at a very high personal cost for some people.

Compassionate people tend to give a great deal to others, in terms of time and physical support but also in terms of emotional support through holding psychological space while listening to the worries and concerns of others. Very often compassionate people give so much to others, they don't put their own needs first.

The costs of compassion can result from negative emotions associated with the perception of letting others down, or from having a lack of boundaries which leaves us feeling as though we are being taken advantage of and not respected. For example: feeling guilty is very common if you feel like you are letting people down, hurting people's feelings or if you say no to a request for help, or even an invite to a party; you might even feel guilty if on occasion you put yourself first. Other uncomfortable emotions including resentment and anger that you might feel towards others (including your partner, friends, your boss, colleagues, neighbours, etc) if you feel you are willingly give up time and energy to others and it either isn't appreciated or reciprocated.

When these difficult emotions show up, we might turn to unhelpful coping strategies, such as comfort eating, alcohol, online shopping, and so on. Some of these strategies can actually be harmful to us because of their negative consequences to health, finances, and so on. As we saw in Growth Zone 5, these strategies exist to numb uncomfortable feelings, quieten the Inner Critic and in essence "switch our brain off", but cause greater harm in the long term if we don't allow emotions and thoughts to be processed properly.

Over time, they can become unhelpful habits and can create dependencies which can be another cost of compassion. These emotions and the unhelpful habits we engage in as a result of them can actually produce physical and emotional pain. These generally manifest as anxiety, stress, depression or overwhelm but can also contribute to chronic illnesses, gastrointestinal problems, exhaustion, fatigue, and so on.

That's why it's so important that we recognise and account for the cost of compassion in our lives. That way we can live up to our core value of caring about others without it damaging ourselves.

Day 19. The Costs of Compassion

The costs of compassion include deeply uncomfortable emotions, unhelpful coping strategies, and quite frequently poor boundaries which result in us being taken advantage of and in some cases treated badly by others.

Many women who are deeply compassionate also identify as 'people-pleasers'. They are the person everyone else comes to because they know you won't let them down. Often, they try to 'fix' people, even if that person hasn't directly asked for help. Compassionate people with poor boundaries can find it impossible to do nothing when listening to other people's problems; it is almost as though there is an unconscious drive to resolve the problems because they simply want to make things better for other people. However, when others don't appreciate, or value those efforts, this can lead quickly to feelings of resentment and anger.

When we feel negative emotions such as guilt or resentment; *and* we continue to put other people's needs first all the time, we are likely to be holding a great deal of negative tension on an ongoing basis. This is very bad for our physical and mental health and cannot be sustained without consequences.

Use the worksheet in the Appendix to help you identify what the costs of compassion are to you. Tomorrow we will look at the consequences of not having good boundaries and learn how to remain compassionate, without allowing ourselves to be treated badly and taken for granted.

Reflection Day 19: To what extent do you identify with some of the negative consequences to yourself, of being a deeply compassionate person?

Day 20. Compassion and People-Pleasing

Yesterday I raised your awareness around the costs of compassion. So often we give our time, love, support and energy to other people and it simply isn't wanted, appreciated, or reciprocated; or in fact valued in any way. When this happens, we might experience some deeply uncomfortable emotions, including resentment and anger towards others (including a partner, friend, boss, colleague, neighbour, etc).

When we feel these difficult emotions, we often try to numb or avoid these feelings by resorting to unhelpful, even harmful coping strategies, such as comfort eating, alcohol, online shopping, smoking, etc. This serves a purpose to numb uncomfortable feelings, quieten the inner critic and in essence "switch our brain off", but causes greater harm in the long term if we don't allow emotions and thoughts to be processed properly.

When we repress our thoughts and emotions, we might also suffer physical and emotional pain, and this will generally show up as anxiety, stress, depression or overwhelm, chronic illnesses, gastrointestinal problems such as IBS, chronic exhaustion, and so on.

Very often people who are deeply compassionate realise that they are people-pleasers - constantly putting other people's needs ahead of their own. By chronically over-giving, they are saying no to their own needs and they are saying no to self-care.

The exercise today will help you to identify when, where and how people-pleasing shows up for you. Follow the worksheet in the Appendix to help you raise your own awareness of your own people-pleasing behaviours. Only when we become fully aware do we become able to start to make change happen. Only then can we start to say 'No' to others, so that we can say 'YES' to ourselves and to the life we want to live.

Reflection Day 20: Do you identify as a 'people-pleaser'? What are the consequences to your own choices when you give so much to others all the time?

Final Day. Review and Future Focus

Day 21. Review of 21 Days to Live Life Stronger

Welcome to the Final Day of the 21 Days to Live Life Stronger; you are so close to the end now! Well done on staying on track and keeping on going until the end.

Today is all about reviewing what you have learnt over the past 21 days and putting in some action to change things for the better. There is no additional activity today, except to have a chance to catch up on any that you have missed and to start to consider what new habits you want to create and what changes you want to make.

As a reminder, the Growth Zones we have explored are:

Growth Zone 1 - Building Healthy Daily Habits and setting small, tiny habits. How has that gone for you? What new habits have you got in place?

Growth Zone 2 - Understanding our Emotions; Why we Feel the Way We Do. Are you better able to identify and understand your emotions and perhaps understand where stress and anxiety come from – could you learn to "love your Chimp"?

Growth Zone 3 - Silencing the Inner Critic. Are you more aware of your inner critic? And how it is more than happy to put you down, criticise you and berate you. Have you noticed how it shows up with your limiting beliefs?

Growth Zone 4 - What is Holding You Back? Limiting Beliefs. Have you started to become aware of the limiting beliefs that are holding you back? Have you tried any of the techniques to transform your limiting beliefs?

Growth Zone 5 - Helpful and Unhelpful Coping Strategies. Can you see how now we numb, avoid, and bury emotions and thoughts with unhelpful coping strategies? What positive, helpful strategies are you using to replace any unhelpful coping strategies you used to have?

Growth Zone 6 - Understanding the Costs of Compassion. And finally, can you start to see what it is costing you to be so compassionate? Is it leading to uncomfortable feelings of guilt, resentment and anger? Is it contributing to your use of harmful coping strategies; and is it causing you emotional and physical pain? If you answer YES to any of these, then it is time to start saying NO to others and start to put your needs first.

If you haven't completed the tasks for each Growth Zone, please do take that opportunity now. This will make up the content for your Personal Toolkit.

When you have completed all the exercises, I would like you to answer the following questions:

1. From all the insights and learning you have gained over the last 21 days, what is the biggest win, or insight that you experienced?
2. From completing the tasks, exercises, and reflections over the course of this programme, what is the ONE thing, that if you changed it today, would have a significant and lasting impact on how you live your life tomorrow, and thereafter?

3. If you implement this ONE thing, what difference do you think it will make to your life? Be specific, be as detailed as possible; really imagine in the minutest detail how your life will be better if you commit to this change.

4. What steps do you commit to, TODAY, to make that change?

Final Review

This final section is all about bringing the learning together. To what extent have you been able to start some new positive daily habits and use them to help you establish a good emotional wellbeing foundation? Similarly, with our positive and helpful coping strategies – to what extent have you been able to strengthen your use of positive coping strategies for prevention or to respond to stress? The better we build our emotional wellbeing foundations, the better able we are able to weather the storms that life inevitably sends our way.

These daily habits and positive coping strategies are the building blocks for a solid foundation. Having a good understanding of why we feel the way we do sometimes (for example, why we feel anxious, or fearful, or overwhelmed) and being prepared to listen to our Chimp and use those emotions as signals that we need to take some action, helps us build that solid foundation using our daily and positive habit building blocks.

When we notice our Inner Critic and we stop it in its tracks, replacing unkind and unjust criticism with self-compassion, then we continue to build our emotional resilience and wellbeing. Equally, when we understand our limiting beliefs, where they came from and how they are holding us back, we empower ourselves to start making lasting changes to our self-beliefs and self-confidence.

Finally, when we understand what it is costing us to be deeply compassionate, we become more willing to make change happen, we become more able to put in boundaries and start saying No to other people, at least some of the time. I am not advocating *not* being compassionate, most would find this an impossible ask anyway, but I am suggesting that we use boundaries and self-care so that we can give wholeheartedly without burning out or breaking down. Some of the costs of compassion will include unhelpful, sometimes harmful, coping strategies and when we are honest with ourselves about the costs and harm we might be causing to ourselves, we become more willing to make change happen.

Your Future Focus

Congratulations and Well Done! You've done it, you've completed the 21 Days to Live Life Stronger book. I hope that you have enjoyed this experience and that you have been able to make the time to learn more about yourself, raise your self-awareness and have learnt some techniques to help you Live Life Stronger. I am passionate about empowering people to live their lives to their full potential, and only when we have great insight into our emotions, thoughts and behaviours, and how to change them, can we really begin to choose our destiny.

The Personal Toolkit in the Appendix will help you to reflect on your main learning points from each Growth Zone and identify any changes you would like to make. Together with your own journalling, you will have given yourself the opportunity to understand yourself at a much deeper level. You will have begun to release the unconscious into conscious thinking.

You may have guessed already, that this book is really just the start of a self-development journey. That was all I ever intended. You only need to perform a simple search and you will find an incredible number of books and resources on daily habits, managing emotions, silencing the Inner Critic, transforming limiting beliefs, coping strategies and people-pleasing. I have included a list of Resources, some of my favourite books and podcasts that I think you will appreciate if you have enjoyed this book.

I hope this 21 Days to Live Life Stronger book has opened your eyes to what has now become possible for you.

Taking this first step to your own self development is one of the most important steps you will ever take. You now have it within you to change your life, and change your future, if you choose to do so.

As a reminder, if you have found it difficult to keep to the daily exercises or would like some help in completing the 21 Day Live Life Stronger Programme, you can access the fully supported online Programme here: https://bit.ly/21DaysLLS. Or scan the QR code below.

I hope that you will continue to practice the techniques you have learned here and that you will now embark on the next stage of this adventure we call Life.

You have one, short, precious life – what will you do with the rest of yours?

APPENDIX

Growth Zone 1. Tools for Positive Healthy Habits

Habit card

This is an example of a habit card I use. Place a tick or cross in the box for each day you complete the habit you want to achieve.

	Mon	Tues	Wed	Thurs	Fri
Habits/ Routines					
Movement/ Exercise					
Quiet time/ Meditation					
Read chapter of book					
Connect with friends/family					
Plan food for today					
Write journal reflection					

Growth Zone 2. Triggers and Stressors Worksheet

The purpose of this worksheet is to help you drill down to what exactly triggers a stress response in you. It's easy to say "I'm stressed" without really understanding what you are 'stressed' about and exactly why you are feeling that way.

When you fully understand *why* and *what* you are stressed about, you can start to take control of your response.

Using the worksheet, answer the following questions:

1.   What situations or people tend to wind you up?
Are there times, places, individuals who you know are going to create challenges for you?

2.   Can you identify how you feel emotionally and physically?
For example, angry, anxious, vulnerable, scared; or something else? You may also get headaches, feel nauseous or get clammy hands. What else happens for you personally?

3.   What typically happens?
Write down a typical example of the event; alternatively write down what is happening for you at the moment if there isn't a 'typical' example.

4.   Then write down what you would like to have happen.
We will return to this later. This is the beginning of you taking control of your response. Maybe you can't immediately see how you can make your desired outcome happen, but over the next 21 days you will start to learn strategies to help you manifest the outcome that you want.

I've used an example here which may help you think about your own triggers and stressors.

My triggers and/or stressors are:

What/who/where	How I feel emotionally and physically	What typically happens	What I'd like to have happen
Example: Regular Monday morning meeting at work	*Example:* Worried; anxious; sick, clammy hands	*Example:* My boss barks orders and generally tells the team what they failed at last week and what we must achieve this week	*Example:* I'd like my boss to tell us what we did well and to negotiate targets.

Growth Zone 3. Inner Critic Worksheet

Write down a situation, or a person, or a goal, where your inner critic shows up (this is also likely to be associated with a limiting belief, see Growth Zone 4).

For example:

Write down some thoughts or beliefs you have where that inner critic shows up with its negative chatter

---

Example:

Whenever I think about going for promotion, I don't really look past the first page of the job spec, I know I won't be good enough. That voice in my head says things like "You know you won't be able to do the job. Why are you even trying? You are not good enough. There are other people much better than you who will apply. Who do you think you are?!"

Now write down where the inner critic shows up for you:

Where else might similar thoughts or beliefs show up? (repeat this as many times as is relevant to you)

Example:

It's not just work, I used to play badminton, but I know I wouldn't be any good at it now. I'd be embarrassed to try, I know I'd be rubbish at it. The chatter in my head says things like "just don't embarrass yourself… you will look a fool, don't kid yourself that you would be any good at badminton now, that was years ago, you are too old and feeble and you will look an idiot on the court"

Now write down where else the inner critic shows up for you

Self-compassion

Imagine a situation where you are with a good friend and they told you they were feeling very low. They tell you they genuinely think they are no good at most things, and that they think they shouldn't try for a job promotion. They feel as if they are unworthy of your friendship and that they have nothing to contribute to the friendship. They feel unattractive, unwanted and unlovable. Thinking about how and where your own inner critic show

Write down what you would say to you friend. Write it here:

Now imagine a time when your inner critic is chattering to you about your 'defects'. Look at what you have said above, now say that to yourself. Write down here some of the self-compassionate things you would say to yourself.

Write about a time, or situation, or relationship where you did well, or tried and succeeded at something. Write about something you are good at or things you have succeeded at (refer also to the Worksheet that comes later entitled "My Timeline"). Think about the skills and abilities you know you have (even if you feel embarrassed to say them or write them down).

Growth Zone 4. Transforming Your Limiting Beliefs Worksheet

There are a number of strategies we can use to overcome and transform our limiting beliefs.

Try to identify where your limiting beliefs show up. It might be at work, in social situations, in relationships. Generally, they do show up all over the place!

Get specific. When you have identified your limiting belief, explore it, and look for contradictory evidence. For example, if you say to yourself, "I always fail", what times have you NOT failed? When and where have you had successes?

If you are stuck on achieving a goal, break it down into the smallest step possible. So for example, if you think you are not good enough to go for a job promotion, why not simply look at the Job Description with a friend; ask them to help you decide whether you could put in an application. Or start listing your strengths before you even look at the job description.

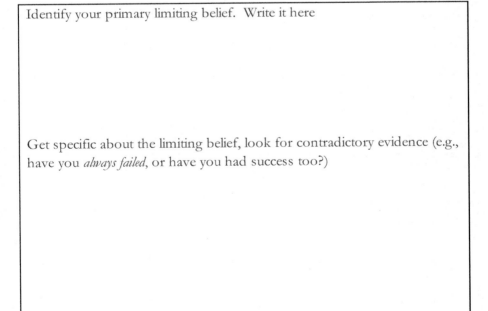

Identify your primary limiting belief. Write it here

Get specific about the limiting belief, look for contradictory evidence (e.g., have you *always failed*, or have you had success too?)

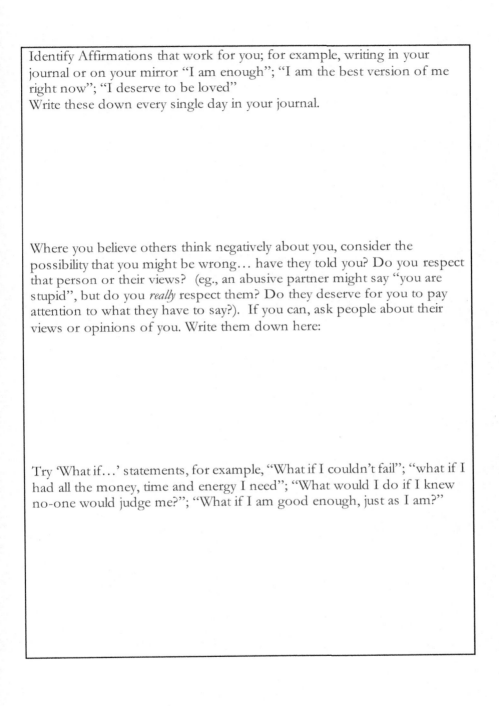

Identify Affirmations that work for you; for example, writing in your journal or on your mirror "I am enough"; "I am the best version of me right now"; "I deserve to be loved"
Write these down every single day in your journal.

Where you believe others think negatively about you, consider the possibility that you might be wrong... have they told you? Do you respect that person or their views? (eg., an abusive partner might say "you are stupid", but do you *really* respect them? Do they deserve for you to pay attention to what they have to say?). If you can, ask people about their views or opinions of you. Write them down here:

Try 'What if...' statements, for example, "What if I couldn't fail"; "what if I had all the money, time and energy I need"; "What would I do if I knew no-one would judge me?"; "What if I am good enough, just as I am?"

Growth Zone 4. Additional Task: Your Timeline/Confidence Board Worksheet

When we feel like our resilience is low, our confidence can feel diminished and our self worth can suffer. It is a useful exercise to have your achievements, or key milestones in one place, do a timeline of all your achievements, or greatest moments. Write down, or draw, something about your greatest achievements and/or the challenges you have overcome.

Writing out your Timeline can be a useful way of transforming some limiting beliefs. When your achievements are written down in front of you, it is hard to hold onto the limiting belief which have no actual evidence to support them – they are just that – a false belief that has become so entrenched that you take it to be true.

When you feel overwhelmed, look at the things you have achieved already. Look at what you have overcome. When life is hard, remember all that you have done before, and that you will do again. However life feels, it will change. Life never stays static.

Growth Zone 5. Unhelpful and Helpful Coping Strategies Worksheet

Unhelpful coping strategies are easy to access at times of acute or chronic stress, they have the fastest and biggest impact. They help us numb our feelings, avoid the thoughts and the problem, and enable us to put up psychological barriers. Whilst they are enticing at the time, they are ultimately unhelpful because they don't give us resources to resolve the problem, they also fail to help up process difficult emotions. They can also lead to addictive and/or dependency issues. Common unhelpful strategies include overuse (or over-control) of food, alcohol, cigarettes, gaming, gambling, sex, drugs (prescription and illegal), self-harm and others. These unskilful strategies then contribute to greater mental health issues such as anxiety and stress and reduce our resilience.

What unhelpful coping strategies do you use?

If you overuse any unhelpful strategies this may be an indication that you need to either; (a) increase your practice of helpful strategies; or (b) take conscious action to reduce your unhelpful coping strategies.

93

Which helpful coping and self-care strategies do you use? What works for you to reduce stress?

If you find yourself using a variety of unhelpful coping mechanisms, then consider what you can do to start changing the balance towards more helpful coping strategies

What new helpful coping strategy could you try?

What could you do more of?

What new strategy will you try out and then practice?

When will you do this?

Growth Zone 6. What Are the Costs of Compassion?   For You Personally.

I don't want anyone to stop being compassionate. Being compassionate is a wonderful quality. Many compassionate people are very happy, and they make others around them very happy too. For the women I work with it is part of who they are; and probably one of their top values. However, I firmly believe that we need to be honest with ourselves with respect to what compassion *costs* us. Because compassion *can and does* come at a very high personal cost for some people.

Here are some of the costs

Unbearable guilt. Perhaps you feel you are letting people down, hurting people's feelings if you say no to a request for help, or even an invite to a party; or feel guilty if on occasion you put yourself first

Deeply uncomfortable emotions, including resentment and anger. Felt towards others (including partner, friends, boss, colleagues, neighbours, etc). Usually felt when you willing give your time and energy to others and it either isn't appreciated or reciprocated. Do you store up repressed emotions, push them down like a beach-ball under the water (See Day 1)?

Unhelpful (even harmful) coping strategies. Comfort eating, alcohol, online shopping, etc. Often hidden. Serves a purpose to numb uncomfortable feelings, quieten the inner critic and in essence "switch our brain off".

Suffer emotional pain. Generally shows up as anxiety, stress, depression or overwhelm.

Suffer physical pain. Headaches, neck pain, back pain, knee pain, foot pain or stomach/digestion problems, eg., IBS; chronic problems, skin rashes/reactions, etc.

Write down here at least 3 'costs' of compassion which show up for you. Write down more as they come to mind.

Are you a people-pleaser? Write down as many ways that this manifests in how you behave towards other people.

What 3 small steps could you start taking today to put boundaries in place, or create some time and space that is just for you?

Growth Zone 6. Understanding Our People-Pleasing Response

In this exercise we are seeking to understand what exactly triggers a people-pleasing response in you. For some people 'people-pleasing' shows up in specific places, for example the workplace, or personal life, with a partner, or parents.

It always shows up around other people (it's an interaction, you can't 'people-please' in isolation)

Using this worksheet, answer the following questions:

1. Where does people-pleasing most show up for you? Give some concrete examples. When was the last time you were really aware that you were 'people-pleasing'?

Specifically:

2. When have you agreed to do something you (honestly) didn't want to do? When did you say 'yes' when you really meant 'NO!'

3. Who did you say this to?

4. How did you feel? Specifically, can you identify how you felt emotionally and physically? For example, anxious, vulnerable, scared, worried you'd be rejected if you didn't do the thing you said you would? You may also experience headaches, feel nauseous or get clammy hands.

5. Did you do the thing you agreed to, or do you find reasons/excuses not to do it.

6. Whether you do the thing you've agreed to, or not, how did you feel?

7. What was the outcome? Did you find reasons/excuses to not do what you had agreed? Did you do it anyway, but feel really resentful about it?

Resources

Books:

Professor Steve Peters (2018). The Chimp Paradox.

Jay Shetty (2020). Think Like a Monk.

James Clear (2018). Atomic Habits

Michael Hyatt (2019). Free to Focus

Podcasts:

Feel Better, Live More. Dr Rangan Chatterjee

On Purpose. Jay Shetty

YouTube:

Marissa Peer

Brendon Burchard

ABOUT THE AUTHOR

Dr Joselyn Sellen is a Chartered Psychologist and Specialist Wellbeing & Resilience Coach. With more than 25 years' experience teaching psychology and promoting wellbeing, she empowers others to make positive choices to promote their psychological wellbeing and fulfil their best potential. Joselyn found her purpose in coaching compassionate people, empowering them to prioritise their own needs and wellbeing in order that they can authentically help others, without experiencing burnout, stress, and compassion fatigue.

www.empoweredchoice.co.uk

Printed in Great Britain
by Amazon

23443231R00066